Bilingual Edition

READING POWER

Edición Bilingüe

EVANDER HOLYFIELD

Heavyweight Champion
Campeón de los pesos pesados

Rob Kirkpatrick

Traducción al español
Mauricio Velázquez de León

The Rosen Publishing Group's
PowerKids Press™ & **Buenas Letras**™
New York

To the reading teacher.
A mi maestro de lectura.

Published in 2002 by The Rosen Publishing Group, Inc.
29 East 21st Street, New York, NY 10010

Copyright © 2002 by The Rosen Publishing Group, Inc.

First Bilingual Edition 2002
First Edition in English 2001

Book design: Maria Melendez

Photo Credits: pp. 5, 7, 9, 11, 21 © Al Bello/Allsport; p. 13 © Ezra Shaw/Allsport; p. 15, 17, 19 © Jed Jacobsohn/Allsport; p. 22 © Elsa Hasch/Allsport.

Text Consultant: Linda J. Kirkpatrick, Reading Specialist/Reading Recovery Teacher

Kirkpatrick, Rob.
    Evander Holyfield : heavyweight champion = Evander Holyfield : campeón de los pesos pesados/ by Rob Kirkpatrick : traducción al español Mauricio Velázquez de León.
    p. cm. — (Reading Power)
    Includes index.
    Summary: Introduces the champion boxer, Evander Holyfield.
    ISBN 0-8239-6148-6
    1. Holyfield, Evander Juvenile literature. 2. Boxers (Sports) — United States Biography Juvenile literature. [1. Holyfield, Evander. 2. Boxers (Sports) 3. Afro-Americans Biography. 4. Spanish language materials—Bilingual.] I. Title. II. Series.
    GV1132.H69 K57 1999
    796.83'092—dc21
    [B]

Word Count:
English: 108
Spanish: 117

Manufactured in the United States of America

Contents ──────

────── Contenido

Evander Holyfield is a boxer.

———

Evander Holyfield es boxeador.

5

Evander boxes in a ring.
Lots of people go to see
him box.

Evander boxea en el
cuadrilátero *(ring)*.
Muchas personas van a
verlo boxear.

Evander wears a robe
before he boxes.

———————

Evander viste una
bata antes de boxear.

9

Boxers fight in rounds. They rest after every round.

Los boxeadores pelean en asaltos (*rounds*). Descansan después de cada asalto.

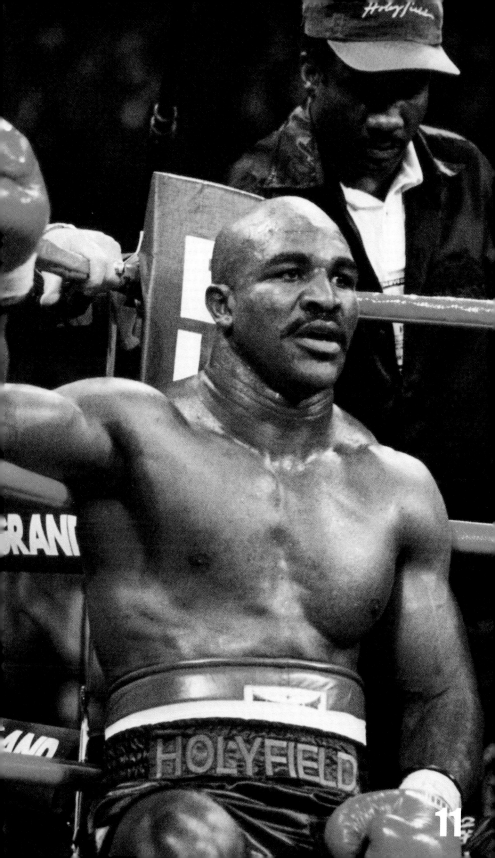

Evander jumps rope.
Jumping rope helps
Evander stay fast.

Evander brinca la cuerda.
Esto lo ayuda a mantener
su velocidad.

In 1996, Evander boxed Mike Tyson.

En 1996, Evander boxeó contra Mike Tyson.

Evander beat Mike Tyson in a fight. Evander was very happy.

Evander le ganó a Mike Tyson. Esta victoria lo puso muy feliz.

When Evander fights Mike Tyson, he has to move fast. Mike throws big punches. Evander throws big punches, too.

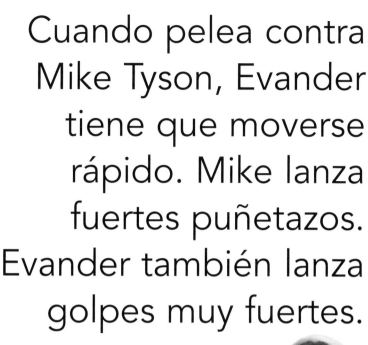

Cuando pelea contra
Mike Tyson, Evander
tiene que moverse
rápido. Mike lanza
fuertes puñetazos.
Evander también lanza
golpes muy fuertes.

Boxers like Evander and Michael Moorer get close in the ring. They keep their gloves up.

Los boxeadores como Evander y Michael Moorer se acercan mucho en el cuadrilátero. Los dos mantienen sus guantes arriba.

Boxers get belts when they win titles. Evander has won lots of belts.

A los boxeadores les dan cinturones cuando ganan títulos. Evander ha ganado muchos cinturones.

Here's a good book to read about boxing:

Para leer más acerca del boxeo, te recomendamos este libro:

Combat Sports (Olympic Sports)
by Robert Sandelson
Crestwood House (1991)

To learn more about boxing, check out this Web site:

Para aprender más sobre boxeo, visita esta página de Internet:

http://www.boxingonline.com

Glossary

belts (BELTS) What boxers get when they win fights.
ring (RING) The place where two boxers fight.
round (ROWND) The time when a boxer boxes in the ring.
title (TY-til) An honor a boxer gets when he is the best.

Index

Glosario

asalto (el) / round El lapso en el que pelea un boxeador.
cinturón (el) Lo que obtienen los boxeadores cuando ganan peleas de campeonato.
cuadrilátero (el) / ring El lugar donde pelean dos boxeadores.
título (el) El honor que obtiene un boxeador cuando es el mejor de su categoría.

Índice